D1450059

Library Media Center
Pleasant Grove Elementary School
Stockbridge, Georgia

Everyday Science Experiments in the Backyard

John Daniel Hartzog

The Rosen Publishing Group's

PowerKids Press™
New York

Library Media Center
Pleasant Grove Elementary School
Stockbridge, Georgia

Some of the experiments in this book are designed for a child to do together with an adult.

Published in 2000 by The Rosen Publishing Group, Inc.
29 East 21st Street, New York, NY 10010 .

Copyright © 2000 by The Rosen Publishing Group, Inc.

All rights reserved. No part of this book may be reproduced in any form without permission in writing from the publisher, except by a reviewer.

Photo Illustrations by Shalhevet Moshe

First Edition

Book Design: Michael de Guzman

Hartzog, John Daniel
      Everyday science experiments in the backyard / by John Daniel Hartzog.
          p.   cm. — (Science surprises)
      Includes index.
      Summary: Provides experiments that explore scientific phenomena occurring in the backyard.
      ISBN 0-8239-5455-2 (alk. paper)
      1. Natural history—Experiments—Juvenile literature. [1. Nature study. 2. Science—Experiments. 3. Experiments.] I. Title. II. Series: Hartzog,
John Daniel. Science surprises.
      QH55.H34   1999
      508—dc21   99-13877
                                                                   CIP

Manufactured in the United States of America

Contents

Science in the Backyard

What does it feel like to be somewhere new for the first time? Is it exciting? Are you curious about the things around you? Sometimes places that you have been to many times before can feel like new places when you look at them in a new way. This book is a collection of **experiments** that will help you to discover new things about familiar places. Taking a "microhike" can make your backyard, your school's field, or a local park into a jungle full of adventure. Exploring at night with a flashlight can open a whole new world. You can even predict the weather! Science helps people find interesting things in familiar places.

Even familiar places like the backyard can be exciting when you look at them through science.

A Microhike

Your backyard is full of wildlife. Sometimes it is hard to see the animals that live in your yard. Many animals are just too small. Let's go on a microhike (a very small hike in a very small area) and see what we can find. To take a microhike we need some string and a magnifying lens. With your string, make a circle on the ground big enough for you to move around in. Step inside the string and kneel down as close to the ground as you can. Now crawl around very slowly.

Materials Needed:
- A long length of string
- A magnifying lens

With the help of a magnifying glass the ground seems to come alive. How many different things can you find? Are there any worms or other bugs? Is there anything growing in the dirt? Take a microhike in different parts of your yard. Do you find different creatures or plants in different places?

You need to get very close to the ground to see all the creatures that live down there. ▶

Materials Needed:
- A glass of milk
- A flashlight

Why Is the Sky Blue?

It's nice to be out in your backyard when the sun is shining and the sky is blue. Have you ever wondered why the sky looks that way? Science will give us the answer.

Sunlight is a mixture of red, orange, yellow, green, blue, indigo, and violet light. Our air is a mixture of many different **particles**. Most light travels through the air in tiny waves that can fit in between the air particles, but the blue and indigo light travel in bigger and longer waves. These waves are so big that the light bumps into the particles and spreads out through the air. When the waves spread out this way, we see a blue sky. Light can make a glass of milk look blue just like it does to the sky. In a dark room, shine a flashlight into a glass of milk. The glass will look blue because the milk particles spread the blue light to the sides.

◀ *Shining a light into a glass of milk can help us understand why the sky is blue.*

Making Dirt and Feeding Worms

Chances are, you've played with dirt and worms in your backyard or at the park. Do you know where dirt comes from? Do you know what worms eat? You can find

Materials Needed:
- A bucket or large pot
- A shovel
- Raw vegetable and fruit scraps

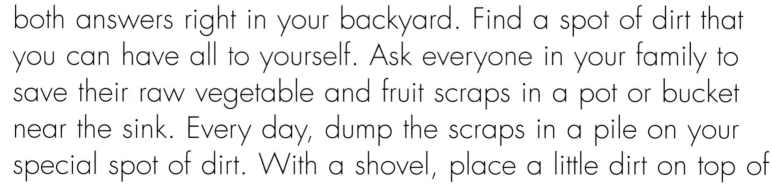

both answers right in your backyard. Find a spot of dirt that you can have all to yourself. Ask everyone in your family to save their raw vegetable and fruit scraps in a pot or bucket near the sink. Every day, dump the scraps in a pile on your special spot of dirt. With a shovel, place a little dirt on top of the pile. As the pile gets bigger, turn over bits of the pile with the shovel until the whole pile is turned over. Do this once every week. The vegetables should start to get mushy and fall apart. After a while, worms will start eating through the vegetables and turn them into dirt. This pile of dirt and vegetables is called **compost**. Compost can help you to feed your garden, and the worms!

This pile of vegetable scraps will become compost over time.

A Leaf Hunt

Materials Needed:
- Leaves
- Papers and pencil

Look around your yard. What is different about the trees you see? Most likely it's the leaves. The shape of a leaf is the best way to **identify** a tree. America is covered with many different kinds of trees. There are oak trees, maple trees, dogwood trees, chestnut trees, and many others. Each **species** of tree has a different shaped leaf.

Collect several different kinds of leaves from your backyard or your neighborhood. Trace the shape of the leaf onto a white sheet of paper. Be careful. Make sure to trace every edge and point of the leaf. When you're finished tracing, send a friend or family member on a leaf hunt. Give her the sheets of paper. Ask her to find a leaf just like the one you have drawn. Then try to find the tree where the leaf came from. Ask your parents to help you identify the tree in a book. You could even make name tags for the trees so everyone will know what kinds of trees they are.

Be careful to trace every edge of the leaves. ▶

Bug Traps

Materials Needed:
- A small shovel
- A large jar (with a wide opening)
- Four small stones
- A piece of wood a little larger than the jar

If you turn over a rock in your backyard, you'll probably find some bugs there. It can be a little creepy when bugs sneak up on you. What if you sneak up on them? Here is a way to make a simple bug trap. Bring your jar out into the yard (or to the park). Dig a hole as big as the jar. Put the jar in the hole so the top is at ground level and surround it with dirt. Place four small stones around the top of the jar. Then rest a piece of wood on top of the stones. The wood should be raised just a little bit over the jar opening.

Step 1

Step 2

Step 3

Small, crawling animals will fit under the wood and fall into the jar. Bugs will not be able to climb the high glass walls so they will be trapped. Check the trap at different times of day. When do you catch the most bugs?

◀ *Don't forget to set the bugs free when you are done.*

Materials Needed:

- A notebook

Tracking Weather

Do you always want to go outside and play? What about when it's raining? Or when it's cloudy? The weather can really change what we do. Now we can even **predict** weather by making **observations**. Looking at the sky and feeling whether it's hot or cold out can help us to guess what the weather will do next. Let's try an experiment. Using your notebook, draw a picture of what you think the sky looks like. Do this twice a day, before school and after school. Write down anything you want to about the weather. Is it cold? Is it raining? After three weeks, you should see a **pattern**. You can use this pattern to predict what the weather will be like later that day or the next.

◀ *You can use your drawings to predict the weather.*

Bird Food

Materials Needed:
- A pie tin
- Birdseed
- A pencil

Do you ever see birds near your house? Most animals are always searching for food. In fact, you can use food to **attract** them to your yard. Here's a way to make sure that birds will come looking for a tasty treat.

Poke tiny holes in the bottom of the pie tin with the point of a pencil (so if it rains, the water will drip out of these holes). Sprinkle some birdseed in the tin. Place the tin on a rock or in a bush in your yard. It may take some time for the birds to find the seeds, so be patient. Soon you will see a variety of birds coming to feed in your backyard. Can you tell which seeds are their favorites? Birds with small beaks will like the small seeds. Birds with larger beaks will be able to eat the larger seeds.

Poking holes in the pie tin will keep the birdseed dry. ▶

Materials Needed:
- A flashlight

Spider Hunting

You probably don't see many spiders in your yard during the day, but have you ever looked at night? On a clear night, take a flashlight into your backyard. Turn it on and hold it against your head, so the light is next to your eye. Slowly, move your eyes and the light together. Shine the light and look under bushes, along fences, and all over your yard. You won't be able to see the spiders, but you will be able to see their eyes! Their eyes will look like little lights sparkling at you. Spiders' eyes need to collect any available light to see well. That is why their eyes sparkle in the light of the flashlight. Slowly walk closer without taking your eyes or the light off the sparkle. As you get closer, you will see the spider.

◀ *Don't move the flashlight as you approach the spider.*

Welcome to Backyard Science

By experimenting with science in your backyard, you have discovered a whole new world. You've made discoveries and seen some of the many different plants and animals that share your backyard. You can understand these things best when you observe them in their own **habitat**. Many of the world's most famous scientists simply watch these living things, just like you did. They measure, they count, they take careful notes, they make experiments. Science is a way of understanding the wonder right in your own backyard.

Glossary

attract (uh-TRAKT) To cause other people, animals, or things to want to be near you.

compost (KAHM-pohst) A mix of decaying animal and vegetable matter.

experiment (ehks-PER-ih-ment) A scientific test designed to answer a question.

habitat (HA-bih-tat) The surroundings where an animal or plant lives.

identify (eye-DENT-ih-feye) To recognize as a specific person or thing. To name something for what it is.

observation (ahb-zer-VAY-shun) To watch closely. To notice something happening.

particle (PAR-tih-kul) A very small piece or part of something.

pattern (PA-turn) An arrangement of shapes, colors, or figures that repeat themselves. A repeated set of characteristics.

predict (pre-DIKT) To try to tell the future. To guess at a possible result.

species (SPEE-sheez) A group of plants or animals that are alike in a specific way.

Index

A
air, 9
animals, 6, 15, 18, 22

B
beaks, 19
birds, 18, 19
bugs, 7, 14, 15

D
dirt, 7, 10, 11

G
garden, 11

L
leaves, 12, 13
light, 9, 21

P
plants, 7, 22

R
rain, 17

S
seeds, 18, 19
sky, 9, 17
spiders, 21

T
trees, 12, 13

V
vegetables, 10, 11

W
waves, 9
weather, 5, 17
wildlife, 6
worms, 7, 10, 11

Web Sites:

You can learn more about science experiments on the Internet. Check out this Web site:
http://www.vickicobb.com